DATE	NAME

COMMENT:

DATE	NAME

COMMENT:

DATE	NAME

COMMENT:

DATE	NAME

COMMENT:

DATE	NAME

COMMENT:

DATE	NAME

COMMENT:

DATE	NAME

COMMENT:

DATE	NAME

COMMENT:

DATE	NAME

COMMENT:

DATE	NAME

COMMENT:

DATE	NAME

COMMENT:

DATE	NAME

COMMENT:

DATE	NAME

COMMENT:

DATE	NAME

COMMENT:

DATE	NAME

COMMENT:

DATE	NAME

COMMENT:

DATE	NAME

COMMENT:

DATE	NAME

COMMENT:

DATE	NAME

COMMENT:

DATE	NAME

COMMENT:

DATE	NAME

COMMENT:

DATE	NAME

COMMENT:

DATE	NAME

COMMENT:

DATE	NAME

COMMENT:

DATE		NAME	

COMMENT:

DATE		NAME	

COMMENT:

DATE		NAME	

COMMENT:

DATE	NAME

COMMENT:

DATE	NAME

COMMENT:

DATE	NAME

COMMENT:

DATE	NAME

COMMENT:

DATE	NAME

COMMENT:

DATE	NAME

COMMENT:

DATE

NAME

COMMENT:

DATE

NAME

COMMENT:

DATE

NAME

COMMENT:

DATE	NAME

COMMENT:

DATE	NAME

COMMENT:

DATE	NAME

COMMENT:

DATE	NAME

COMMENT:

DATE	NAME

COMMENT:

DATE	NAME

COMMENT:

DATE

NAME

COMMENT:

DATE

NAME

COMMENT:

DATE

NAME

COMMENT:

DATE	NAME

COMMENT:

DATE	NAME

COMMENT:

DATE	NAME

COMMENT:

DATE

NAME

COMMENT:

DATE

NAME

COMMENT:

DATE

NAME

COMMENT:

DATE	NAME

COMMENT:

DATE	NAME

COMMENT:

DATE	NAME

COMMENT:

DATE

NAME

COMMENT:

DATE

NAME

COMMENT:

DATE

NAME

COMMENT:

DATE	NAME

COMMENT:

DATE	NAME

COMMENT:

DATE	NAME

COMMENT:

DATE	NAME

COMMENT:

DATE	NAME

COMMENT:

DATE	NAME

COMMENT:

DATE	NAME

COMMENT:

DATE	NAME

COMMENT:

DATE	NAME

COMMENT:

DATE	NAME

COMMENT:

DATE	NAME

COMMENT:

DATE	NAME

COMMENT:

DATE:

NAME:

COMMENT:

DATE:

NAME:

COMMENT:

DATE:

NAME:

COMMENT:

DATE	NAME

COMMENT:

DATE	NAME

COMMENT:

DATE	NAME

COMMENT:

DATE

NAME

COMMENT:

DATE

NAME

COMMENT:

DATE

NAME

COMMENT:

DATE

NAME

COMMENT:

DATE

NAME

COMMENT:

DATE

NAME

COMMENT:

DATE	NAME

COMMENT:

DATE	NAME

COMMENT:

DATE	NAME

COMMENT:

DATE	NAME

COMMENT:

DATE	NAME

COMMENT:

DATE	NAME

COMMENT:

DATE	NAME

COMMENT:

DATE	NAME

COMMENT:

DATE	NAME

COMMENT:

DATE

NAME

COMMENT:

DATE

NAME

COMMENT:

DATE

NAME

COMMENT:

DATE

NAME

COMMENT:

DATE

NAME

COMMENT:

DATE

NAME

COMMENT:

DATE	NAME

COMMENT:

DATE	NAME

COMMENT:

DATE	NAME

COMMENT:

DATE	NAME

COMMENT:

DATE	NAME

COMMENT:

DATE	NAME

COMMENT:

DATE

NAME

COMMENT:

DATE

NAME

COMMENT:

DATE

NAME

COMMENT:

DATE	NAME

COMMENT:

DATE	NAME

COMMENT:

DATE	NAME

COMMENT:

DATE	NAME

COMMENT:

DATE	NAME

COMMENT:

DATE	NAME

COMMENT:

DATE:

NAME:

COMMENT:

DATE:

NAME:

COMMENT:

DATE:

NAME:

COMMENT:

DATE	NAME

COMMENT:

DATE	NAME

COMMENT:

DATE	NAME

COMMENT:

DATE	NAME

COMMENT:

DATE	NAME

COMMENT:

DATE	NAME

COMMENT:

DATE	NAME

COMMENT:

DATE	NAME

COMMENT:

DATE	NAME

COMMENT:

DATE:

NAME:

COMMENT:

DATE:

NAME:

COMMENT:

DATE:

NAME:

COMMENT:

DATE	NAME

COMMENT:

DATE	NAME

COMMENT:

DATE	NAME

COMMENT:

DATE:

NAME:

COMMENT:

DATE:

NAME:

COMMENT:

DATE:

NAME:

COMMENT:

DATE	NAME

COMMENT:

DATE	NAME

COMMENT:

DATE	NAME

COMMENT:

DATE

NAME

COMMENT:

DATE

NAME

COMMENT:

DATE

NAME

COMMENT:

DATE	NAME

COMMENT:

DATE	NAME

COMMENT:

DATE	NAME

COMMENT:

DATE

NAME

COMMENT:

DATE

NAME

COMMENT:

DATE

NAME

COMMENT:

DATE	NAME

COMMENT:

DATE	NAME

COMMENT:

DATE	NAME

COMMENT:

DATE	NAME

COMMENT:

DATE	NAME

COMMENT:

DATE	NAME

COMMENT:

DATE	NAME

COMMENT:

DATE	NAME

COMMENT:

DATE	NAME

COMMENT:

DATE		NAME	

COMMENT:

DATE		NAME	

COMMENT:

DATE		NAME	

COMMENT:

DATE

NAME

COMMENT:

DATE

NAME

COMMENT:

DATE

NAME

COMMENT:

DATE		NAME	

COMMENT:

DATE		NAME	

COMMENT:

DATE		NAME	

COMMENT:

DATE	NAME

COMMENT:

DATE	NAME

COMMENT:

DATE	NAME

COMMENT:

DATE	NAME

COMMENT:

DATE	NAME

COMMENT:

DATE	NAME

COMMENT:

DATE	NAME

COMMENT:

DATE	NAME

COMMENT:

DATE	NAME

COMMENT:

DATE

NAME

COMMENT:

DATE

NAME

COMMENT:

DATE

NAME

COMMENT:

DATE

NAME

COMMENT:

DATE

NAME

COMMENT:

DATE

NAME

COMMENT:

DATE

NAME

COMMENT:

DATE

NAME

COMMENT:

DATE

NAME

COMMENT:

DATE	NAME

COMMENT:

DATE	NAME

COMMENT:

DATE	NAME

COMMENT:

DATE	NAME

COMMENT:

DATE	NAME

COMMENT:

DATE	NAME

COMMENT:

DATE	NAME

COMMENT:

DATE	NAME

COMMENT:

DATE	NAME

COMMENT:

DATE	NAME

COMMENT:

DATE	NAME

COMMENT:

DATE	NAME

COMMENT:

DATE	NAME

COMMENT:

DATE	NAME

COMMENT:

DATE	NAME

COMMENT:

DATE	NAME

COMMENT:

DATE	NAME

COMMENT:

DATE	NAME

COMMENT:

DATE	NAME

COMMENT:

DATE	NAME

COMMENT:

DATE	NAME

COMMENT:

DATE	NAME

COMMENT:

DATE	NAME

COMMENT:

DATE	NAME

COMMENT:

DATE

NAME

COMMENT:

DATE

NAME

COMMENT:

DATE

NAME

COMMENT:

DATE	NAME

COMMENT:

DATE	NAME

COMMENT:

DATE	NAME

COMMENT:

www.ingramcontent.com/pod-product-compliance
Ingram Content Group UK Ltd.
Pitfield, Milton Keynes, MK11 3LW, UK
UKHW052121230426
12049UKWH00010BA/145